BIRTHDAYS AND ANNIVERSARIES

Images by

ANNE GEDDES

ISBN 1-55912-001-0

© Anne Geddes 1994

Published in 1995 by Cedco Publishing Company,
2955 Kerner Blvd, San Rafael, CA 94901.

First USA edition, January 1995
Second printing, February 1995
Third printing, September 1995

Designed by Jane Seabrook
Produced by Kel Geddes
Color separations by Metro Repro
Artwork by Bazz 'n' Else
Printed through Colorcraft, Hong Kong

ANNE GEDDES

Anne Geddes, an Australian-born photographer, resident in Auckland, New Zealand, has won the hearts of people internationally with her unique and special images of children.

Not only is her work widely recognized and sought after in the commercial field, but her exceptional images have received resounding critical acclaim, attracting a host of professional awards.

Many of Anne's distinctive and memorable photographs have been published internationally, including the prestigious USA's *"Life"* Magazine, Germany's *"Tempo"*, the *"London Sunday Mirror"* and The News of the World *"Sunday Magazine"* to name but a few.

Anne's work mirrors the joy and love found in the children who will form the future of the planet. After all, she says, *"To be able to capture on film the innocence, trust and happiness that is inherent in the next generation is a very special responsibility. It's work that rewards me daily with a great deal of personal satisfaction."*

Another major challenge in Anne's life is to ensure that the photography of children is widely accepted as an art form that legitimately competes with any other form of photographic speciality.

Anne is married to her friend and business partner Kel. Together they have two children.

CONTENTS

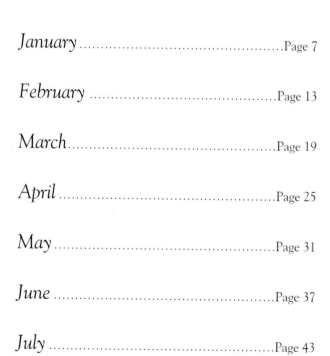

JANUARY

Birthdays

Name _____

Birth date _____

Star sign _____

Gift ideas _____

Name _____

Birth date _____

Star sign _____

Gift ideas _____

Name _____

Birth date _____

Star sign _____

Gift ideas _____

Name _____

    Birth date _____

       Star sign _____

        Gift ideas _____

          Name _____

           Birth date _____

           Star sign _____

          Gift ideas _____

Birthdays

Name

Birth date

Star sign

Gift ideas

Name

Birth date

Star sign

Gift ideas

Name

Birth date

Star sign

Gift ideas

Name

Birth date

Star sign

Gift ideas

Name

Birth date

Star sign

Gift ideas

Birthdays

Name _____

Birth date _____

Star sign _____

Gift ideas _____

Name _____

Birth date _____

Star sign _____

Gift ideas _____

Name _____

Birth date _____

Star sign _____

Gift ideas _____

Name _____

Birth date _____

Star sign _____

Gift ideas _____

Name _____

Birth date _____

Star sign _____

Gift ideas _____

Anniversaries

Name

Date

Occasion

Name

Date

Occasion

Name

Date

Occasion

Name

Date

Occasion

Name

Date

Occasion

Name

Date

Occasion

Special Occasions

Name

Date

Occasion

Name

Date

Occasion

Name

Date

Occasion

Name

Date

Occasion

Name

Date

Occasion

Name

Date

Occasion

FEBRUARY

Birthdays

Name _____

Birth date _____

Star sign _____

Gift ideas _____

Name _____

Birth date _____

Star sign _____

Gift ideas _____

Name _____

Birth date _____

Star sign _____

Gift ideas _____

Name _____

Birth date _____

Star sign _____

Gift ideas _____

Name _____

Birth date _____

Star sign _____

Gift ideas _____

Birthdays

Name

Birth date

Star sign

Gift ideas

Name

Birth date

Star sign

Gift ideas

Name

Birth date

Star sign

Gift ideas

Name

Birth date

Star sign

Gift ideas

Name

Birth date

Star sign

Gift ideas

Birthdays

Name ⎯⎯⎯⎯⎯⎯⎯⎯⎯⎯⎯⎯⎯⎯⎯⎯⎯⎯⎯⎯⎯⎯

Birth date ⎯⎯⎯⎯⎯⎯⎯⎯⎯⎯⎯⎯⎯⎯⎯⎯⎯⎯

Star sign ⎯⎯⎯⎯⎯⎯⎯⎯⎯⎯⎯⎯⎯⎯⎯⎯⎯⎯⎯

Gift ideas ⎯⎯⎯⎯⎯⎯⎯⎯⎯⎯⎯⎯⎯⎯⎯⎯⎯⎯⎯

Name ⎯⎯⎯⎯⎯⎯⎯⎯⎯⎯⎯⎯⎯⎯⎯⎯⎯⎯⎯⎯⎯⎯

Birth date ⎯⎯⎯⎯⎯⎯⎯⎯⎯⎯⎯⎯⎯⎯⎯⎯⎯⎯

Star sign ⎯⎯⎯⎯⎯⎯⎯⎯⎯⎯⎯⎯⎯⎯⎯⎯⎯⎯⎯

Gift ideas ⎯⎯⎯⎯⎯⎯⎯⎯⎯⎯⎯⎯⎯⎯⎯⎯⎯⎯⎯

Name ⎯⎯⎯⎯⎯⎯⎯⎯⎯⎯⎯⎯⎯⎯⎯⎯⎯⎯⎯⎯⎯⎯

Birth date ⎯⎯⎯⎯⎯⎯⎯⎯⎯⎯⎯⎯⎯⎯⎯⎯⎯⎯

Star sign ⎯⎯⎯⎯⎯⎯⎯⎯⎯⎯⎯⎯⎯⎯⎯⎯⎯⎯⎯

Gift ideas ⎯⎯⎯⎯⎯⎯⎯⎯⎯⎯⎯⎯⎯⎯⎯⎯⎯⎯⎯

Name ⎯⎯⎯⎯⎯⎯⎯⎯⎯⎯⎯⎯⎯⎯⎯⎯⎯⎯⎯⎯⎯⎯

Birth date ⎯⎯⎯⎯⎯⎯⎯⎯⎯⎯⎯⎯⎯⎯⎯⎯⎯⎯

Star sign ⎯⎯⎯⎯⎯⎯⎯⎯⎯⎯⎯⎯⎯⎯⎯⎯⎯⎯⎯

Gift ideas ⎯⎯⎯⎯⎯⎯⎯⎯⎯⎯⎯⎯⎯⎯⎯⎯⎯⎯⎯

Name ⎯⎯⎯⎯⎯⎯⎯⎯⎯⎯⎯⎯⎯⎯⎯⎯⎯⎯⎯⎯⎯⎯

Birth date ⎯⎯⎯⎯⎯⎯⎯⎯⎯⎯⎯⎯⎯⎯⎯⎯⎯⎯

Star sign ⎯⎯⎯⎯⎯⎯⎯⎯⎯⎯⎯⎯⎯⎯⎯⎯⎯⎯⎯

Gift ideas ⎯⎯⎯⎯⎯⎯⎯⎯⎯⎯⎯⎯⎯⎯⎯⎯⎯⎯⎯

Anniversaries

Name

Date

Occasion

Name

Date

Occasion

Name

Date

Occasion

Name

Date

Occasion

Name

Date

Occasion

Name

Date

Occasion

Special Occasions

Name _____

Date _____

Occasion _____

Name _____

Date _____

Occasion _____

Name _____

Date _____

Occasion _____

Name _____

Date _____

Occasion _____

Name _____

Date _____

Occasion _____

Name _____

Date _____

Occasion _____

MARCH

Birthdays

Name _____

Birth date _____

Star sign _____

Gift ideas _____

Name _____

Birth date _____

Star sign _____

Gift ideas _____

Name _____

Birth date _____

Star sign _____

Gift ideas _____

Name _____

Birth date _____

Star sign _____

Gift ideas _____

Name _____

Birth date _____

Star sign _____

Gift ideas _____

Birthdays

Name

Birth date

Star sign

Gift ideas

Name

Birth date

Star sign

Gift ideas

Name

Birth date

Star sign

Gift ideas

Name

Birth date

Star sign

Gift ideas

Name

Birth date

Star sign

Gift ideas

Birthdays

Name _____

Birth date _____

Star sign _____

Gift ideas _____

Name _____

Birth date _____

Star sign _____

Gift ideas _____

Name _____

Birth date _____

Star sign _____

Gift ideas _____

Name _____

Birth date _____

Star sign _____

Gift ideas _____

Name _____

Birth date _____

Star sign _____

Gift ideas _____

Anniversaries

Name

Date

Occasion

Name

Date

Occasion

Name

Date

Occasion

Name

Date

Occasion

Name

Date

Occasion

Name

Date

Occasion

Special Occasions

Name

Date

Occasion

Name

Date

Occasion

Name

Date

Occasion

Name

Date

Occasion

Name

Date

Occasion

Name

Date

Occasion

APRIL

Birthdays

Name _____

Birth date _____

Star sign _____

Gift ideas _____

Name _____

Birth date _____

Star sign _____

Gift ideas _____

Name _____

Birth date _____

Star sign _____

Gift ideas _____

Name _____

Birth date _____

Star sign _____

Gift ideas _____

Name _____

Birth date _____

Star sign _____

Gift ideas _____

Birthdays

Name

Birth date

Star sign

Gift ideas

Name

Birth date

Star sign

Gift ideas

Name

Birth date

Star sign

Gift ideas

Name

Birth date

Star sign

Gift ideas

Name

Birth date

Star sign

Gift ideas

Name _____

Birth date _____

Star sign _____

Gift ideas _____

Name _____

Birth date _____

Star sign _____

Gift ideas _____

Name _____

Birth date _____

Star sign _____

Gift ideas _____

Name _____

Birth date _____

Star sign _____

Gift ideas _____

Name _____

Birth date _____

Star sign _____

Gift ideas _____

Anniversaries

Name

Date

Occasion

Name

Date

Occasion

Name

Date

Occasion

Name

Date

Occasion

Name

Date

Occasion

Name

Date

Occasion

Special Occasions

Name

Date

Occasion

Name

Date

Occasion

Name

Date

Occasion

Name

Date

Occasion

Name

Date

Occasion

Name

Date

Occasion

MAY

Birthdays

Name _____

Birth date _____

Star sign _____

Gift ideas _____

Name _____

Birth date _____

Star sign _____

Gift ideas _____

Name _____

Birth date _____

Star sign _____

Gift ideas _____

Name _____

Birth date _____

Star sign _____

Gift ideas _____

Name _____

Birth date _____

Star sign _____

Gift ideas _____

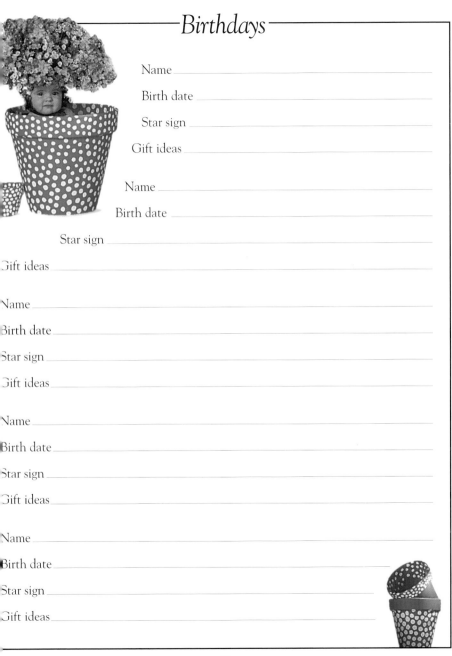

Birthdays

Name

Birth date

Star sign

Gift ideas

Name

Birth date

Star sign

Gift ideas

Name

Birth date

Star sign

Gift ideas

Name

Birth date

Star sign

Gift ideas

Name

Birth date

Star sign

Gift ideas

Birthdays

Name _____

Birth date _____

Star sign _____

Gift ideas _____

Name _____

Birth date _____

Star sign _____

Gift ideas _____

Name _____

Birth date _____

Star sign _____

Gift ideas _____

Name _____

Birth date _____

Star sign _____

Gift ideas _____

Name _____

Birth date _____

Star sign _____

Gift ideas _____

Anniversaries

Name

Date

Occasion

Name

Date

Occasion

Name

Date

Occasion

Name

Date

Occasion

Name

Date

Occasion

Name

Date

Occasion

Special Occasions

Name

Date

Occasion

Name

Date

Occasion

Name

Date

Occasion

Name

Date

Occasion

Name

Date

Occasion

Name

Date

Occasion

JUNE

Birthdays

Name

Birth date

Star sign

Gift ideas

Name

Birth date

Star sign

Gift ideas

Name

Birth date

Star sign

Gift ideas

Name

Birth date

Star sign

Gift ideas

Name

Birth date

Star sign

Gift ideas

Birthdays

Name

Birth date

Star sign

Gift ideas

Name

Birth date

Star sign

Gift ideas

Name

Birth date

Star sign

Gift ideas

Name

Birth date

Star sign

Gift ideas

Name

Birth date

Star sign

Gift ideas

Birthdays

Name

Birth date

Star sign

Gift ideas

Name

Birth date

Star sign

Gift ideas

Name

Birth date

Star sign

Gift ideas

Name

Birth date

Star sign

Gift ideas

Name

Birth date

Star sign

Gift ideas

Anniversaries

Name

Date

Occasion

Name

Date

Occasion

Name

Date

Occasion

Name

Date

Occasion

Name

Date

Occasion

Name

Date

Occasion

Special Occasions

Name

Date

Occasion

Name

Date

Occasion

Name

Date

Occasion

Name

Date

Occasion

Name

Date

Occasion

Name

Date

Occasion

July

Birthdays

Name

Birth date

Star sign

Gift ideas

Name

Birth date

Star sign

Gift ideas

Name

Birth date

Star sign

Gift ideas

Name

Birth date

Star sign

Gift ideas

Name

Birth date

Star sign

Gift ideas

Birthdays

Name

Birth date

Star sign

Gift ideas

Name

Birth date

Star sign

Gift ideas

Name

Birth date

Star sign

Gift ideas

Name

Birth date

Star sign

Gift ideas

Name

Birth date

Star sign

Gift ideas

Birthdays

Name _____

Birth date _____

Star sign _____

Gift ideas _____

Name _____

Birth date _____

Star sign _____

Gift ideas _____

Name _____

Birth date _____

Star sign _____

Gift ideas _____

Name _____

Birth date _____

Star sign _____

Gift ideas _____

Name _____

Birth date _____

Star sign _____

Gift ideas _____

Anniversaries

Name

Date

Occasion

Name

Date

Occasion

Name

Date

Occasion

Name

Date

Occasion

Name

Date

Occasion

Name

Date

Occasion

Special Occasions

Name _____

Date _____

Occasion _____

Name _____

Date _____

Occasion _____

Name _____

Date _____

Occasion _____

Name _____

Date _____

Occasion _____

Name _____

Date _____

Occasion _____

Name _____

Date _____

Occasion _____

AUGUST

Birthdays

Name

Birth date

Star sign

Gift ideas

Name

Birth date

Star sign

Gift ideas

Name

Birth date

Star sign

Gift ideas

Name

Birth date

Star sign

Gift ideas

Name

Birth date

Star sign

Gift ideas

Birthdays

Name

Birth date

Star sign

Gift ideas

Name

Birth date

Star sign

Gift ideas

Name

Birth date

Star sign

Gift ideas

Name

Birth date

Star sign

Gift ideas

Name

Birth date

Star sign

Gift ideas

Birthdays

Name

Birth date

Star sign

Gift ideas

Name

Birth date

Star sign

Gift ideas

Name

Birth date

Star sign

Gift ideas

Name

Birth date

Star sign

Gift ideas

Anniversaries

Name

Date

Occasion

Name

Date

Occasion

Name

Date

Occasion

Name

Date

Occasion

Name

Date

Occasion

Name

Date

Occasion

Special Occasions

Name _____

Date _____

Occasion _____

Name _____

Date _____

Occasion _____

Name _____

Date _____

Occasion _____

Name _____

Date _____

Occasion _____

Name _____

Date _____

Occasion _____

Name _____

Date _____

Occasion _____

SEPTEMBER

Birthdays

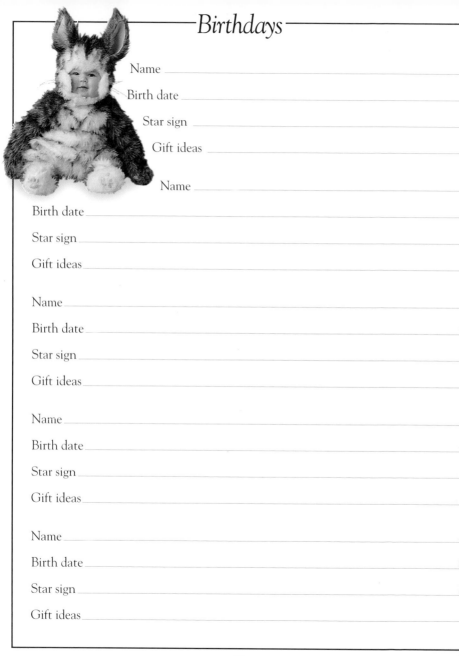

Name _____

Birth date _____

Star sign _____

Gift ideas _____

Name _____

Birth date _____

Star sign _____

Gift ideas _____

Name _____

Birth date _____

Star sign _____

Gift ideas _____

Name _____

Birth date _____

Star sign _____

Gift ideas _____

Name _____

Birth date _____

Star sign _____

Gift ideas _____

Birthdays

Name

Birth date

Star sign

Gift ideas

Name

Birth date

Star sign

Gift ideas

Name

Birth date

Star sign

Gift ideas

Name

Birth date

Star sign

Gift ideas

Name

Birth date

Star sign

Gift ideas

Birthdays

Name _____

Birth date _____

Star sign _____

Gift ideas _____

Name _____

Birth date _____

Star sign _____

Gift ideas _____

Name _____

Birth date _____

Star sign _____

Gift ideas _____

Name _____

Birth date _____

Star sign _____

Gift ideas _____

Name _____

Birth date _____

Star sign _____

Gift ideas _____

Anniversaries

Name

Date

Occasion

Name

Date

Occasion

Name

Date

Occasion

Name

Date

Occasion

Name

Date

Occasion

Name

Date

Occasion

Special Occasions

Name

Date

Occasion

Name

Date

Occasion

Name

Date

Occasion

Name

Date

Occasion

Name

Date

Occasion

Name

Date

Occasion

OCTOBER

Birthdays

Name _____

Birth date _____

Star sign _____

Gift ideas _____

Name _____

Birth date _____

Star sign _____

Gift ideas _____

Name _____

Birth date _____

Star sign _____

Gift ideas _____

Name _____

Birth date _____

Star sign _____

Gift ideas _____

Name _____

Birth date _____

Star sign _____

Gift ideas _____

Birthdays

Name

Birth date

Star sign

Gift ideas

Name

Birth date

Star sign

Gift ideas

Name

Birth date

Star sign

Gift ideas

Name

Birth date

Star sign

Gift ideas

Name

Birth date

Star sign

Gift ideas

Birthdays

Name _____

Birth date _____

Star sign _____

Gift ideas _____

Name _____

Birth date _____

Star sign _____

Gift ideas _____

Name _____

Birth date _____

Star sign _____

Gift ideas _____

Name _____

Birth date _____

Star sign _____

Gift ideas _____

Name _____

Birth date _____

Star sign _____

Gift ideas _____

Anniversaries

Name

Date

Occasion

Name

Date

Occasion

Name

Date

Occasion

Name

Date

Occasion

Special Occasions

Name

Date

Occasion

Name

Date

Occasion

Name

Date

Occasion

Name

Date

Occasion

Name

Date

Occasion

Name

Date

Occasion

NOVEMBER

Name _____

Birth date _____

Star sign _____

Gift ideas _____

Name _____

Birth date _____

Star sign _____

Gift ideas _____

Name _____

Birth date _____

Star sign _____

Gift ideas _____

Name _____

Birth date _____

Star sign _____

Gift ideas _____

Name _____

Birth date _____

Star sign _____

Gift ideas _____

Birthdays

Name

Birth date

Star sign

Gift ideas

Name

Birth date

Star sign

Gift ideas

Name

Birth date

Star sign

Gift ideas

Name

Birth date

Star sign

Gift ideas

Name

Birth date

Star sign

Gift ideas

Birthdays

Name

Birth date

Star sign

Gift ideas

Name

Birth date

Star sign

Gift ideas

Name

Birth date

Star sign

Gift ideas

Name

Birth date

Star sign

Gift ideas

Name

Birth date

Star sign

Gift ideas

Anniversaries

Name _____

Date _____

Occasion _____

Name _____

Date _____

Occasion _____

Name _____

Date _____

Occasion _____

Name _____

Date _____

Occasion _____

Name _____

Date _____

Occasion _____

Name _____

Date _____

Occasion _____

Special Occasions

Name

Date

Occasion

Name

Date

Occasion

Name

Date

Occasion

Name

Date

Occasion

Name

Date

Occasion

Name

Date

Occasion

DECEMBER

Birthdays

Name _____

Birth date _____

Star sign _____

Gift ideas _____

Name _____

Birth date _____

Star sign _____

Gift ideas _____

Name _____

Birth date _____

Star sign _____

Gift ideas _____

Name _____

Birth date _____

Star sign _____

Gift ideas _____

Name _____

Birth date _____

Star sign _____

Gift ideas _____

Merry
Christmas
to you.

Birthdays

Name

Birth date

Star sign

Gift ideas

Name

Birth date

Star sign

Gift ideas

Name

Birth date

Star sign

Gift ideas

Name

Birth date

Star sign

Gift ideas

Name

Birth date

Star sign

Gift ideas

Birthdays

Name _____

Birth date _____

Star sign _____

Gift ideas _____

Name _____

Birth date _____

Star sign _____

Gift ideas _____

Name _____

Birth date _____

Star sign _____

Gift ideas _____

Name _____

Birth date _____

Star sign _____

Gift ideas _____

Anniversaries

Name

Date

Occasion

Name

Date

Occasion

Name

Date

Occasion

Name

Date

Occasion

Name

Date   Occasion

Special Occasions

Name

Date

Occasion

Name

Date

Occasion

Name

Date

Occasion

Name

Date

Occasion

Name

Date

Occasion

Name

Date

Occasion

STAR SIGNS,
ANNIVERSARIES,
BIRTHSTONES
&
FLOWERS.

AQUARIUS *21 January – 19 February*

Eccentric, uncompromising, unconventional and unpredictable, Aquarians hate pretense. They are great intellectual snobs, but they're definitely not social ones and instead are often committed humanitarians with strong social and political consciences. In fact their love for people in general often overrides their love of individuals, and they are hard to get to know intimately and find difficulty forming long-term relationships. They love to argue, and will come up with innovative ideas but they fall short in applying them. They are natural performers. In their desire for freedom, they tend to shun the constraints of conventional marriages.

Perfect partner: Scorpio.

Disasters: Cancer.

PISCES *20 February – 20 March*

The original chameleons, elusive Pisceans constantly change their feelings and ideas and will see something of value in everything – even opposites. They are very intuitive, sensitive and idealistic, but often lack common sense. They hate confrontations, and have the knack of seeming compliant while continuing to do exactly as they please. They can become visionaries or mystics, but at their worst may embrace the escapism offered by drugs or alcohol. They are great romantics, known for their desire to see everything through rose-colored glasses, but in their search for an ideal soul mate they are frequently drawn to domineering types.

Perfect partners: Capricorn, Taurus.

Disasters: Gemini.

ARIES *21 March – 20 April*

Optimistic, assertive and lively, Arians throw themselves headlong at life. They know what they want, and they want it immediately and will pursue their ambition relentlessly. They hate delays, and can be impatient and intolerant. They have strong egos and need new challenges and constant flattery to be really happy. They hate to take advice and can be bossy, but will never bear grudges. Their generous and bawdy natures make them fun companions, but if they feel excitement is lacking, you can rely on them to generate a few crises to liven things up!

Perfect partner: Gemini.

Disasters: Cancer.

TAURUS *21 April – 20 May*

Gentle, affectionate and conservative, Taureans love their homes and families above all else. They are not terribly ambitious and their cautious natures thrive under routine. They can be snobbish and are great social climbers but are poor judges of character. They are masters of self-restraint, but underlying that placid facade is an extremely sensuous nature, that often finds release in a tendency for laziness and a love of good food. Relationships are a priority for Taureans, and they fall in love easily and passionately. If love goes wrong, they will often persevere, and remain in loveless marriages.

Perfect partner: Cancer.
Disasters: Scorpio.

GEMINI *21 May – 21 June*

The proverbial split personality, Geminis treasure clarity and reason. Often highly strung, Geminis are always overloaded with countless projects, none of which they explore in any depth. Their ready wit and lively minds make them popular, but often they are lacking in the long-term commitment that's necessary to make lasting friendships. Don't expect them to keep a secret – they love gossip and are always ready for a discussion as long as it's not about their emotions. They can be moody and emotionally immature. They need some freedom to be happily married and partners should be prepared for them to indulge in a few dalliances.

Perfect partner: Libra.
Disasters: Virgo.

CANCER *22 June – 22 July*

Caring, considerate and committed, Cancers seem made for the institution of marriage. They love their homes and are often great hoarders. Underneath their tough shells they are highly sensitive emotionally, and can easily feel rejected. They grow stronger when faced with adversity. They are often very sensual, but they try to hide their feelings from all but a privileged few. They are tenacious, and can be calculating. Don't expect them to spill the beans the first time you meet them – they'll hold themselves in check till they're sure you're worth the commitment, then attach themselves to you with Superglue! They are incredibly loyal and loving partners, even when the going gets tough.

Perfect partners: Taurus, Leo.
Disasters: Sagittarius, Aquarius.

LEO *23 July – 22 August*

Warm, creative and generous, Leos demand the lion's share of attention. They crave constant approval and have a strong urge for self-expression – many end up in the theater and those who don't still act as if they are stars. They need to achieve their goals to be happy, and if thwarted or angered can be deadly. Some Leos are overconfident and vain, but equally many are truly charismatic. Leos are moody and veer to extremes. If they don't acquire some self-knowledge they can be strident egotists. They plunge into love affairs, and usually have plenty of admirers if they learn not to be too overbearing.

Perfect partners: Gemini, Cancer.
Disasters: Capricorn.

VIRGO *23 August – 22 September*

Thoughtful, meticulous and critical, Virgos seem to have invented the word perfectionist. With their eye for detail and conscientious natures, they will accept only the highest of standards in everything. Because of this they have a tendency to be workaholics and are motivated by a strong sense of duty. They love gossip and their sharp wit can be malicious. Because of their tendency to rationalize, they often find relationships difficult, and will analyze everything to the enth degree. They usually marry late, and often never walk down the aisle, but once committed make dependable, caring and considerate companions.

Perfect partners: Cancer, Taurus.
Disasters: Sagittarius.

LIBRA *23 September – 22 October*

Charming, graceful, fair-minded Librans often top the popularity polls, and they make a special effort to present a smiling face to the world. They are diplomatic, and will go out of their way to avoid arguments in their constant search for harmony in all things. This can make them seem a little bland or two-faced at times, but they are only trying to please everyone all the time. They suppress anger, and this often leads to stress-related illnesses. They love things of beauty and will make an extra effort to get the means to afford an elegant lifestyle. Having a partner is an essential for Librans, and although they are very accommodating they like to feel they are in control emotionally.

Perfect partners: Librans will make a go of any relationship but Sagittarius is an especially good combination.

SCORPIO *23 October – 22 November*

Strong, resourceful Scorpios are personalities of extremes. They are able to endure physical and emotional hardships and their behavior can fluctuate from spiritual to debauched. Their intense natures thrive on crises, which give them the opportunity to let off steam, and they are often their own worst enemies. They make devoted and committed friends, but if they scent betrayal, beware – they make relentless foes. They can be moody, but thrive in a loving, secure environment. They are known for their strong sexual energy but cherish a relationship that is equally as stimulating mentally and spiritually.

Perfect partners: Cancer, Libra.

Disasters: Aries, Gemini, Scorpio.

SAGITTARIUS *23 November – 23 December*

Friendly, open, generous and vibrant, Sagittarians can be guaranteed to liven up any occasion. If they offend you with their frank remarks, remember that they are rarely malicious, and that they suffer from speak–first–and–think–later syndrome. They are always travelling in a bid to ease those ever–itchy feet. They love to mix with the "in" crowd and can be rather snobbish. They hate any restraint on their ebullient spirits and though they'll run through lovers at a rate of knots, they'll be very reticent about tying themselves to any one person.

Perfect partners: Virgo, Libra.

Disasters: Cancer, Scorpio.

CAPRICORN *23 December – 20 January*

Determined, practical and reliable, Capricorns will reach the positions of power and authority they crave no matter what. Their ambitions can lead them to be opportunistic and domineering, but underneath their stern facades they are often just great big softies. Although they seem reserved, if they're surrounded by friends you could be surprised by how decadent and outgoing they are. They are natural leaders and hate being subservient, though given power they can be tyrannical. They are artistic and frequently become involved in some sort of spiritual quest. They make loyal, faithful companions, although they're often a little emotionally insensitive.

Perfect partners: Virgo, Taurus.

Disasters: Gemini.

ANNIVERSARIES

1st	Paper	13th	Lace
2nd	Cotton	14th	Ivory
3rd	Leather	15th	Crystal
4th	Silk or Flowers	20th	China
5th	Wood	25th	Silver
6th	Iron or Candy	30th	Pearl
7th	Copper or Wool	35th	Coral
8th	Bronze or Rubber	40th	Ruby
9th	Pottery	45th	Sapphire
10th	Tin	50th	Gold
11th	Steel	55th	Emerald
12th	Linen	60th	Diamond

Birthstones

January	Garnet – Constancy and truth
February	Amethyst – Sincerity, humility
March	Aquamarine – Courage and energy
April	Diamond – Innocence, success
May	Emerald – Tranquillity
June	Pearl – Precious, pristine
July	Ruby – Carefree, chaste
August	Moonstone – Joy
September	Sapphire – Hope, chastity
October	Opal – Reflects every mood
November	Topaz – Fidelity, loyalty
December	Turquoise – Love and success

Flowers

January	Snowdrop – Pure and gentle
February	Carnation – Bold and brave
March	Violet – Modest
April	Lily – Virtuous
May	Hawthorn – Bright and hopeful
June	Rose – Beautiful
July	Daisy – Wide-eyed and innocent
August	Poppy – Peaceful
September	Morning Glory – Easily contented
October	Cosmos – Ambitious
November	Chrysanthemum – Sassy and cheerful
December	Holly – Full of foresight

GIFT LIST

Name _____ Date _____   Name _____ Date _____

Gift _____   Gift _____

Name _____ Date _____   Name _____ Date _____

Gift _____   Gift _____

Name _____ Date _____   Name _____ Date _____

Gift _____   Gift _____

Name _____ Date _____   Name _____ Date _____

Gift _____   Gift _____

Name _____ Date _____   Name _____ Date _____

Gift _____   Gift _____

Name _____ Date _____   Name _____ Date _____

Gift _____   Gift _____

Name _____ Date _____

Gift _____

Name _____ Date _____

Gift _____

Name _____ Date _____

Gift _____

Name _____ Date _____

Gift _____

Name _____ Date _____ Name _____ Date _____
Gift _____ Gift _____

Name _____ Date _____ Name _____ Date _____
Gift _____ Gift _____

Name _____ Date _____ Name _____ Date _____
Gift _____ Gift _____

Name _____ Date _____ Name _____ Date _____
Gift _____ Gift _____

Name _____ Date _____ Name _____ Date _____
Gift _____ Gift _____

Name _____ Date _____ Name _____ Date _____
Gift _____ Gift _____

Name _____ Date _____ Name _____ Date _____
Gift _____ Gift _____

Name _____ Date _____ Name _____ Date _____
Gift _____ Gift _____

Name _____ Date _____ Name _____ Date _____
Gift _____ Gift _____

Name _____ Date _____ Name _____ Date _____
Gift _____ Gift _____

Name _____ Date _____ Name _____ Date _____
Gift _____ Gift _____

CHRISTMAS LIST

Name _____ Year _____   Name _____ Year _____
Gift _____   Gift _____

Name _____ Year _____   Name _____ Year _____
Gift _____   Gift _____

Name _____ Year _____   Name _____ Year _____
Gift _____   Gift _____

Name _____ Year _____   Name _____ Year _____
Gift _____   Gift _____

Name _____ Year _____   Name _____ Year _____
Gift _____   Gift _____

Name _____ Year _____   Name _____ Year _____
Gift _____   Gift _____

Name _____ Year _____   Name _____ Year _____
Gift _____   Gift _____

Name _____ Year _____   Name _____ Year _____
Gift _____   Gift _____

Name _____ Year _____   Name _____ Year _____
Gift _____   Gift _____

Name _____ Year _____   Name _____ Year _____
Gift _____   Gift _____